Let's read and talk a... Internet Safety

Anne Rooney

W

First published in 2011 by Franklin Watts

Franklin Watts
338 Euston Road, London NW1 3BH

Franklin Watts Australia
Level 17/207 Kent St, Sydney, NSW 2000

Created by Taglines Creative Ltd:
www.taglinescreative.com
Series designer: Hayley Cove
Editor: Jean Coppendale

Series literacy consultant: Kate Ruttle is a freelance literacy consultant and Literacy
Co-ordinator, Special Needs Co-ordinator and Deputy Head at a primary school in Suffolk

ISBN: 978 1 4451 0391 4
Dewey classification: 004.6'78
A CIP catalogue for this book is available from the British Library

Picture credits
t=top b=bottom l=left r=right
Cover images: front Mandy Godbehear/Shutterstock; back Rob Marmion/Shutterstock
Series icons: books, Osa, dddelli, Jut/Shutterstock; speech bubbles, Dic Liew/Shutterstock;
Computer screen, ildogesto/Shutterstock;
6 AVAVA/Shutterstock; 7 Marco Mayor/Shutterstock; 8 Adisa/Shutterstock;
9 iofoto/Shutterstock; 10 Andi Berger/Shutterstock; 11 Flirt/SuperStock; 12 Elena
Elisseeva/Shutterstock; 13 Rob Marmion/Shutterstock; 14 Rob Marmion/Shutterstock;
15 Cultura Limited/SuperStock; 16 Supri Suharjoto/Shutterstock; 17 MaszaS/Shutterstock;
18 thumb/Shutterstock; 19 Monkey Business Images/Shuttestock; 20 Disney Club
Penguin/SuperStock; 21 Rob Marmion/Shutterstock; 22 Monkey Business
Images/Shutterstock; 23 Monkey Business Images/Shutterstock; 24 IndexStock/SuperStock;
25 Monkey Business Images/Shutterstock; 26 Arvind Balaraman/Shutterstock; 27 Leah-Anne
Thompson/Shutterstock

Every attempt has been made to clear copyright on the photographs used in this book.
Should there be any inadvertent omission please apply to the publisher for rectification.

Printed in China

Franklin Watts is a division of Hachette Children's Books, an Hachette UK company.
www.hachette.co.uk

Contents

Pages marked with ⬇ have a free downloadable activity sheet at www.franklinwatts/downloads Find out more on page 30.

Words in **bold** are in the glossary on page 29.

What can I do on the internet?

The **internet** offers great ways to learn new things and keep in touch with people you know, but you need to be careful.

What can I do online?

There's a lot you can do online, such as play games, chat with friends, listen to music and watch videos. You might join a **social networking** site, use websites to help with your homework, or share your artwork and photos with friends. Perhaps you use email to send messages to your friends and family, too.

You can use the internet to chat with friends, do school research and watch videos.

Where can I use computers to go on the internet?

You might use a computer at home to go online, or a computer at school or in a library. Some people have phones that connect to the internet. You can also use your phone to send text messages, and to take and share pictures and videos.

How can I meet people online?

There are lots of ways of meeting other people online. You might make friends and share news, photos and web links on a social networking site. You can play games with other people. Some social networking and games pages have a 'chat' window which you can use to chat in text to your friends online.

Talk about

✪ How do you and your friends use computers and phones to keep in touch? Do you share pictures and videos?

You can use some phones to go online.

Do I need to be careful online?

As in real life, you need to be careful about people and places you don't know.

Who might I meet online?

Online you may meet people you don't know. On the internet it's hard to tell if someone is really who they say they are. Some people whom you meet online may not be nice. They may say they're your friend, but remember that you don't really know them.

You wouldn't walk off with someone you didn't know on the street – you should be just as careful online.

Why do I have to be careful about meeting new people online?

You can't see who you're talking to online so people can lie about who they are. Sometimes an older person might pretend to be a child to get you to be their friend, or another child might pretend to be someone they are not. Most people only want to have fun online but a few might say or do nasty things.

Talk about

✪ **How do you think you can avoid unkind people getting in touch with you?**

✪ **What would you do if someone sent you a nasty message?**

Someone may write and tell you they're your age but really they are much older.

Are all web pages okay to look at?

The internet is for adults as well as children so there are web pages that are not suitable for children. You need to be careful what you look at (see pages 20–21).

Is sharing online safe?

It's good fun to share with friends, and this is safe to do if you keep some things private.

What should I keep private?
It's best to keep your most personal news and photos to share just with friends you know well in real life. You don't need to give your address or other contact details, your age or date of birth on a social networking site.

Keep pictures of you and your family private and only share them with people you know.

Can I control who sees my stuff?

You can set **privacy settings** on your own pages on social networking sites. These let you choose who can see your photos, **status updates** and videos. Make sure details and photos that show where you live and which school you go to are kept private.

Taking videos is a great way to keep in touch with friends and family who live far away.

TAKE ACTION

Check your privacy settings on any site you share with friends. Make sure strangers can't see your stuff. Ask a grown-up to help change your settings if you need to.

What if someone won't share with me?

You can't insist that someone sends you a photo or gives you their personal details – they're just being careful.

Talk about

✪ Who are you happy to share your photos and videos with?

✪ How would you feel if someone you don't know was looking at your photos and reading about what you're doing?

How can I be a good online friend?

It just takes a little thought to be a good online friend to people you know and to new friends.

Should I post photos and videos of others online?
If you want to **tag** other people in photos or videos, always ask them first, and don't do it if they don't want you to. If there is a funny photo you want to **post**, think for a minute – will it upset or embarrass someone to have the photo online?

Make sure you have everyone's permission before you put pictures or a video online.

Do I have to be a 'friend' to people who ask me?

You don't have to be friends online with people you don't know well or don't like, but try not to upset them. If you don't want to be online friends, just ignore the request or send a polite message saying you're only 'friends' with people you know well.

If you're not sure about someone, you don't have to be friends with them.

Talk about

✪ What would you do if someone your friends know, but you don't know, asked to be your friend online?

✪ What would you do if you asked someone to be your online friend and they don't want to?

What if I upset someone?

Try not to make jokes about groups of people or write nasty things even if you think you're doing it in fun. If you do upset someone by mistake, always say you're sorry.

Is it safe to chat online?

Talking to friends online is fun – but be very careful what you say to people you don't know well.

Where can I chat online?

You can often chat on game sites such as Club Penguin, on a social networking site or a site that uses a special chat **program**. If you want to chat on a website make sure it's a space for children and has a **moderator**.

Ask an adult to check if a chat site has a moderator – someone who keeps an eye on everything to keep you safe.

Should I use my real name on a chat website?

It's best to use a nickname when you chat, so that people who don't know you can't find out who you are. Don't give out your real name to strangers, or tell anyone where you live, which school you go to, or give them your phone number or other contact details.

Use video chat with people you know well.

Talk about

- ✪ **If you're chatting online with someone and they say or do something that makes you feel upset or uncomfortable, what can you do?**

Is video chat safe?

If your computer has a **webcam**, you might be able to use video chat. Only ever use video chat with people you know really well, such as a parent or a brother or sister.

Do I need to be careful using email?

Email is a good way to keep in touch with friends and family but you still need to be careful.

Who can I email safely?

You might like to use email to keep in touch with friends or family, but it's not a good idea to email people you don't know. If you get an email from someone you've never heard of it might be **spam**. If you're not sure about an email ask a grown-up for advice or delete it unopened. It may contain a **virus**.

Family and friends who live far away will enjoy receiving emails.

Is it safe to open files with emails?

Files sent with emails can also contain a virus that can cause lots of problems with your computer. Your computer may have anti-virus software to protect it but this might not stop new viruses coming through. It's best not to open attachments from people you don't know, either.

Is sending information by email safe?

Email is a good way to share photos and news. Remember, however, that people can easily pass on or post online anything you send with an email.

Talk about

✪ Which people would you be happy sending emails to and getting emails from?

✪ Why would you be happy to open emails and files they send you?

Sending your holiday photos to your family by email is easy — but remember they might show them to their friends!

How can I keep my personal spaces safe?

You will need to **log in** to use your personal space on a website or chat – this helps to keep your space safe.

Should I keep my **password** secret? Yes! If someone knows your password, they can put up or delete pictures and information on your page, and send messages that look as if they came from you. If they send nasty messages to people you know, or upload something horrid, you could get into trouble.

Log in

Username: **********

Password: **************

Log in

You need a password to open your pages and to post updates, photos and messages.

TAKE ACTION

Are the passwords you use secret enough? Change any you're not sure about and keep a note of them somewhere safe that is nowhere near the computer.

How do I choose a good password?

Choose a password that you can remember but that other people can't guess – so not your pet's name, for example, or the date of your birthday! Use a mix of letters and numbers as that is harder to guess.

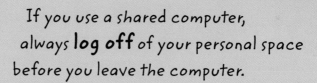

Talk about

⭐ Why isn't it a good idea to use the same password for everything?

⭐ What are some ways to keep your login details safe?

If you use a shared computer, always **log off** of your personal space before you leave the computer.

How do I keep my password safe?

When you are keying in your password make sure no one is standing behind you. Don't save your login details on a computer at school, in the library or at a friend's house. Log off your pages when you've finished. If someone finds out your password, change it straight away.

Does it matter which web pages I look at?

There are websites on all sorts of subjects, but some web pages might frighten you or show you something nasty.

How do I know which websites are safe to visit?

Try to use a website you know – if you go to the CBeebies site or Club Penguin, there will be no unpleasant surprises. Ask your friends about websites they know and enjoy or that are good for homework.

Websites such as Club Penguin, run by Disney, are good fun.

Is it safe to search?

Look for a **search page** made for children where you will find information that is right for you. These search pages won't show links to anything that is scary or unsuitable.

Talk about

- ✪ How do you find out about websites that are okay to use?

- ✪ What would you do if you accidentally found a nasty website?

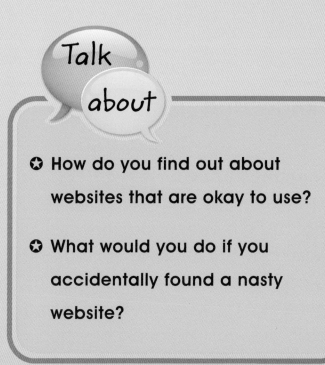

Ask an adult to check out a website if you're not sure about it.

Is free stuff safe?

Some pages offer lots of free stuff, such as ring tones and backgrounds. These pages sometimes put extra bits of bad software on your computer. To be safe ask a grown-up to download and check out any free stuff you want.

TAKE ACTION Make a list of the top ten favourite websites of your friends for fun and homework.

21

Do I need to be careful about my mobile?

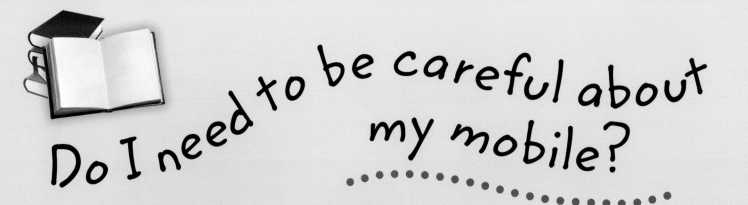

Only give your mobile telephone number to people you know and trust.

How can my phone be a problem?
Some people might use your phone as a way of being mean to you. They may send you nasty text messages or make unkind phone calls. They may phone during the night to wake you up or during classes to get you into trouble at school.

Only give your number to close friends and family and then you can enjoy all your text messages.

What if I'm already having problems?

If someone you liked before has started being unkind to you, tell a grown-up. Keep any nasty messages to show to the grown-up. Most phones let you **block** calls and messages from a particular number. You can also change your number easily and it doesn't cost anything.

Ask before taking someone's photo and before sharing it.

Talk about

✪ Have you ever had an upsetting text or voice message? What did you do about it?

✪ What would you do if someone showed you a photo or video that made someone look silly or that would upset them?

Can I share photos and videos taken on my phone?

Always ask other people in the photo if they are okay about sharing the photo. Don't take photos of someone being hurt or crying, and don't join in if other people are doing it.

23

What is a cyberbully?

Someone who uses technology, such as mobile phones and computers, to bully other people is a cyberbully.

What can a cyberbully do?

A bully on the computer or on the phone can't kick you or pull your hair. But they can send you text messages that upset or frighten you, post nasty comments about you or put up photos that make you look silly.

TAKE ACTION

Lots of schools have a bullying charter. Find out what your school bullying charter says about **cyberbullying**. If it doesn't seem very good, your class might be able to suggest something better.

Making lots of nasty phone calls to someone is a form of cyberbullying.

Who becomes a cyberbully?

Cyberbullies usually know the people they bully. Sometimes, other people join in without knowing how hurtful they are being or because they're scared not to. Some people don't mean to be bullies, but they become bullies by taking part.

Cyberbullies often bully the same people in real life.

Talk about

❂ **If your friends were leaving someone out of a group activity such as a game, or making unkind comments about them online, what would you do?**

Can you bully someone by doing nothing?

Deliberately leaving someone out of activities, or not letting them join an online game or chat, can be just as hurtful as saying nasty things about them.

What if something bad happens online?

Even if you're careful, things can sometimes go wrong when you're online. If something bad happens tell an adult straight away.

What if someone is nasty to me?

If someone writes on your page or comments on your photos in ways you don't like, don't respond. Block them and stop being their online friend. If you get a nasty email or text message, don't reply. Don't answer calls from someone who is being mean to you.

You can always block someone from your pages if they are being nasty.

What if someone asks to meet me?

You might feel you have really got to know someone you have met online and that you have a lot in common, but never agree to meet them unless a grown-up goes with you. You can't be sure they are really nice and they might want to do some bad things.

How do I report bad things?

Lots of web pages have a button to 'Report **abuse**'. You can use this if someone says something nasty. Deleting things that upset you means you don't have to see them but it's best to show them to a grown-up you trust first, and ask for help.

Press delete if something upsets you but show it to a grown-up first.

Talk about

- ✪ How have you dealt with any problems online?

- ✪ Who would you talk to if you had a problem?

Talk about

✪ How do you choose who to add as friends online? If you get a friend request from someone you don't know in the real world, should you ever add them?

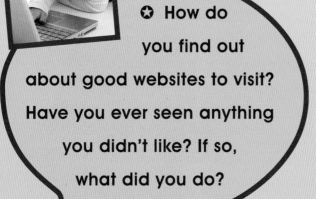

✪ Which search pages do you use? Do they just show you safe and suitable links?

✪ How do you find out about good websites to visit? Have you ever seen anything you didn't like? If so, what did you do?

✪ What do you know about making privacy settings on websites where you post your news and pictures? Is your stuff hidden from strangers?

Note to parents

Parental involvement and responsibility are essential in keeping children safe on the internet. To find out how to set up safe searching on a real search engine go to:

http://www.google.co.uk/familysafety/

Make sure the firewall on the computer your child uses is enabled.

Be safe when you're searching

Here is a list of child-friendly search engines:

www.yahooligans.com
www.msn.co.uk/kids
www.kidsclick.org
www.askforkids.com

Glossary

abuse unkind behaviour

block stop someone sending you messages

chat a conversation carried out in text by typing in a message window on the computer

cyberbullying using computers and mobile phones to upset and scare someone

email mail messages sent by computer

internet network of computers joined together around the world that can share information

log in give your user name and password so that you can use your own pages or account on a website, on a mobile phone or on a computer

log off/log out close the connection with your pages or account on a website or the computer

moderator an adult whose job it is to make sure that a chatsite is safe for children to use

online connected to the internet

password secret word that you need to use to log on to your computer or web pages

post put something online on a website, such a picture or message

privacy settings settings you can make to control who can look at your text and pictures on a website

program a piece of software that instructs your computer and mobile phone to do something, such as run a game or let you write a text

search page web page used to look for information by searching other web pages

social networking sharing news and photos with other people online

software instructions the computer follows to carry out a task, such as showing web pages or letting you write a story

spam unwanted email sent to lots of people at once

status updates short line on a social networking site such as Bebo that tells people what you are doing or thinking

tag add someone's name to a picture or video

virus small program that causes harm to a computer and is passed between computers, rather like the computer catching an illness

webcam short for web camera, which is connected to your computer so that the video is sent straight to a web page or chat session

Index

Activity sheets

The following spreads have accompanying worksheets, which are available to download for free at www.franklinwatts.co.uk

What can I do on the internet? (pages 6–7)
There are so many terms to get used to in the cyber world. This activity sheet challenges children to remember what all the terms mean.

How can I keep my personal spaces safe? (pages 18–19)
A handy sheet of dos and don'ts for creating and keeping passwords safe.

What if something bad happens online? (pages 26–27)
This sheet presents several scenarios of things that have happened to children online. What would they do in each case?